IMPRESSION

To Nikki
Thank you so much for
your support! I hope
you enjoy reading this
⌐"⌐

IMPRESSION

POEMS

CHARNJIT GILL

Escape here....

Lots of love
From
Charnjit
x x x x

atmosphere press

CONTENTS

OURSELVES

OUR FAITH

IF LIFE IS A DREAM

Then why does it feel like a nightmare

                  A nightmare you can't wake up from

If life is a dream

                  Then what is reality?

If life is a dream

                  Are we asleep?

                  Or are we awake?

If life is a dream,

Am I life's dream?

Or is life my dream?

FAITH FORMATION

Faith and devotion are how life is constructed
Faith lights the way

Truth and compassion are how it is conducted

Happiness and humility are how we've been instructed

The pursuit of happiness is a human one

Mortals should be merry

we are imperfect

but we can be in good spirit

People want to be pleased

we are souls that want to smile

fundamentally we want to have fun

we can be socially sunny

we are compassionate

so we want others to be content too

Individual joy can be infectious

glee can make us more carefree

we are delighted

beaming with pride

grinning from ear to ear

We glow differently

There is gratitude in satisfaction

Blessings radiate out

It can be thrilling, exhilarating, an ecstatic experience that is

euphoric

Overjoyed with rapture

Oh the oblivion

because love cannot be reconstructed

LOVE THE SINNER, HATE THE SIN

We love the sinner
We hate the sin

We love mischief
but hate the grin

We love voodoo dolls
but hate the pins

We love the body
but hate the skin

We love the winner
but hate the win

We love the outside
but hate within

AGNOSTIC

stop expecting
miracles
from people who
don't believe in
God

its fraud

you don't need a
nod of approval
it's odd
to plod along
when people keep

prodding you

is this your squad?
if not, don't applaud

MOVE

People don't leave

     God moves them

because they have proved what they needed to you

God approved everything

     so, everything is to improve you

          so, God removes people

as a countermove

               to your disapproval

GOD'S PLAN

A door that you didn't see before

God takes away people or things to add
someone or something to your life

Once the purpose of anything is served – it stops
God ends things

To begin something else

God hears you even if you're not listening

God does things in his way
not yours

Happiness might not be with the people you think

God looks for you
even if you don't see him

When God leaves you alone
in the dark

It's to remind you that he is the light
to guide you

to inspire you
Let God rearrange things

Change things for the better
Count on God

You'll lose count of how many times he's been there for you
Sometimes you rely on your faith

instead of facts

We encounter problems

to have enough wisdom for the solution
God is constant

Don't be inconsistent

HOLD

Hope only makes you wait
It doesn't change reality

You sightsee a different life
It makes you think about how things could be

but there's no guarantee

It appeals to you
but that doesn't mean you can achieve it

It's a belief you have
that you want to complete

An ideal scenario
that is waiting to be released

You'll be relieved is it does
because it's so surreal

Hold onto

                                        hope

It's the only thing

            that will help you

                                        cope

AFFLUENCE

It doesn't matter how much money you have in the bank

You'll always

    be rich

    in blessings

HEAVENLY HUSTLE

Find your heavenly hustle

Flex your divine muscles

Let the angels tussle

THE END

What if we get to the end and the fat lady doesn't sing?

What will we do then?

24 HOURS

Abstract nights

make concrete days

OUR RELATIONSHIPS

TOO LOUD

We will always be too loud
                        for a world
that never intended
                        on listening to
                                    us

Too much noise like sitting on a bus

                        causing a fuss
seeing it as a plus

                        instead of sitting down to discuss

                                    they haven't got the

                                    guts to

                                                hear it

BOUND

We're bound up by calendars, reminders and to do lists
we struggle to fit fun things in

a holiday
a new restaurant
catch up with friends
watch a film

Our priorities takeover the present, we pin hopes onto the future
One day it will fit in the puzzle of life

organised
well placed

COMPANY

Hang out with people
                    who fit your future
not your history
The future is a mystery
especially when the present is slippery
but victory is always on the periphery
The company around you can make it a special delivery

to your future

VALIDATION

We seek validation from people

               that aren't

                    valid

We balance

      the malice with our

               emotional palette

           questioning our talent

REAL PEOPLE

Telling people they are   wrong

may earn you enemies

but when people realise that you are

                                                                right

You might earn some

                                                                friends

COURAGE

Courage is where one person takes

                               our rage

to say and do what we are afraid of

That's

                               outrage

Courage doesn't come with

                               age

It comes with company

SEE

Some people see you
Some people see your
                    baggage

Either way they decide
whether they can handle it

because it comes as one
                    package

Even if it's damage
Instead of dragging it
It's a challenge
but you can manage

to salvage
the undamaged

RECIPROCATE

Feelings go both ways
If they don't
reciprocate, they don't
deserve it
Its concern
to deter you
from disturbing yourself
Divert your attention
observe
Reserve it for yourself

Don't absorb
Don't let it disturb you
explore your emotions
ignore what you don't need
implore to see reason
Build rapport
remorse what can't reward
Support yourself
so you can transform

TRY

Sometimes we try for people who don't try for us

it's not worth the fuss

If we continue to

      then

            We're

            stuck

            in a rut

CONNECTION

Sometimes love is
dressed up as special
connections and attraction

but it's only worth it if you act
Otherwise it's a distraction

We want a reaction

An emotional transaction that we get through interaction
that's what brings satisfaction

your absence is felt

by the

      lack of

         passion

IMPORTANT

We all want to be missed

It means that we are important

      to someone

We affected them

PLAYERS

Players become toys
to someone else's game

They only have

     themselves to

          blame

RIGHT ONE

Stop chasing the wrong one

                                  The right one won't
                      run

If they run

     They're not

            The one

ATTACHMENTS

Maybe we don't get attached to people

we get attached to how they make us feel when

        we are around them

we can deal with anything

they make us feel like we're healing even if we're not
heartbroken

On the days, we're left reeling

they make them seem appealing

they steal   our sadness

but they never   reveal it

They have a way of getting to the

        depths of

        our personality

without

breaking down

our walls

        or peeling

PART

Having a part to play in someone's life is both overwhelming and liberating

it's about waiting

as it is about dictating

it can be devastating

or fascinating

it can be motivating

or suffocating

but having a chance is exhilarating

invigorating

because you're participating

MEANT

His stars weren't meant for   my sky

His soul wasn't meant for   my eyes

RELATIONSHIP STORIES

People talk about their relationships as stories

> It's a long story
> It's complicated

but what about if your love life was a short story?

Only with one or two characters

not as complicated but

> just as cagey

where she called him Babe and he called her Baby

It was love at first sight – Crazy

they saw each other

> Daily

Lots of decisions were

> Hasty

Their memory of it

> Hazy

Things started changing lately

It got

> Shady

> Shaky

but that's their memory of it

    Vaguely

TIME WHISPERS

Time whispered

        you

           out of my life

If time is money

Then

    both

      have been

        cut

          out of my life

MOMENT

I want to take this moment

to climb into your heart

It's the only way

I can stop myself

from

falling apart

INHERIT

What we inherit

It can seem like a Gift from Heaven
but it's got 'her' in it

because she's a Parent
        a Mum

because her Presence
        is a Present

So, who are we to discredit?

That's why she gets all our merits

        It's one hell of a job

What we owe our mothers is a debt that can never be repaid

There comes a time when they cut the apron strings,
but we still remember the blade

it's a memory that doesn't fade
a mother's lessons are taught every day

we attended all the classes
but we're not sure if we make the grade

        Look at the life they made for us

Working hard so they can be paid
for the food in our stomachs
the clothes on our backs
and a roof over our head

If life is a game, they've been playing for so long that it'll be
a while before we get played

They've prayed for us
we might be their sunshine
but they are our shades

When you've got Queens of Hearts as mothers, what are
you going to do with Spades?

Life is a narrow path
but mothers were there
every time we strayed
every time we swayed
When everyone else left, they stayed

When we thought we had the world on our shoulders

they had it weighed

told us not to be afraid

that when things go down, it can really cascade

there's been many times that we have left them dismayed

but there's a lot that goes on behind the display

Our mistakes are downplayed

They are our first aid

a patient grenade

it's handmade

it's homemade

Mothers invade our lives

to help us find something that we've
mislaid

They want us to be an upgrade of them

Someday

it might not be today

But that's the thing,

a mother's love ricochets anyway

STOP

Stop telling women they are broken

Stop telling us that we need to look for another half

a better half

Stop telling us that we're whole
We know

If we are broken
it's because of the men that have broken us

we think that we can help them
we can heal them

so, either we stay
or we try to make them to

It's supposed to empower us
yet it takes the power away from us

Stop dictating to us what we're supposed to think what
we're supposed to feel

Stop mansplaining our hearts to us
When you don't understand its craft

so, you know women
Dated
Some
Engaged to some
Married some

so, she became your first draft

but relationships are hard graft

They require effort from both sides
so, stop telling us that we're weak

Stop telling us to be strong
Stop telling us to be soft in a hard world
Stop telling us to toughen up in this soft world

Stop telling us

QUICK FIX

Quick fixes don't last

they do what is asked

but it

     runs out

               fast

PURGATORY

After
        the love of

        her life
                        died

She had

        no heart

                        for the living

OURSELVES

FREE

Set yourself free

for me

STRONG

If you want to be strong, learn

    how to be alone

It shows how much you've grown

    own it

Make it your home

    compose yourself

    control yourself

SOLITUDE

Solitude

      makes us

            sweeter and safer

You

      learn to

            handle things

LONER

Sometimes you're supposed to be a loner

        because no one really understands you

The more people you spend time with, the more you lose yourself

    you'll do it

    because you must

        maybe you want to

    but you're afraid of

        ending up like

            everyone else

ALONE

The loneliest people

    are the lonely people

        that don't look lonely

            They live boldly
           but if you look closely

           They're very homely
              almost holy

         in their own matrimony

INTUITION

Intuition is the navigation of the soul
It only works if you listen and

                                    go

SHIFT

We mould
We evolve
We dream
We grow

We experience change

A shift where time
shapes you

Changes your expectations

through:

> lessons,
> hardships,
> heartache
> laughter

Reflect on yourself

Listen to yourself

You think and feel that way for a reason
What's right is unique to the individual

Bloom into yourself

CHANGE

We want change
Positive change

We don't want to react to everything
we wish we didn't care as much about everything so much

It seems like it would make things easier
We want to be able to decide better what we give our energy
to

How is it received?
Is it reciprocated?

We want to able to make decisions
to feel good about making it

As well as dealing with the consequences of it
Whatever it may be

We want to
            change
            but

            we don't know how

We have the power
            and possibilities,
            but

it paralyses us

To the point of powerlessness

ANGEL'S ANGLES

Stop waiting for angels
Start looking for angles
change your point of view

Review the journey you are on regularly

Look at the specifics particularly

POTENTIAL

Exceed your potential

You are

more than

your credentials

Pursuing your passion

is essential

even if it's confidential

It can

become influential

even

experimental

It makes you gentle

It makes you special

MORE

If you see me less, I'm doing more
I'm opening doors of opportunities

I'm pouring myself into life
doing more than I'm asked for

more than ever before

I'm exploring

SEE FAILURE

to succeed

Look at your failures

Failure is feedback

it cracks your capability

It is a knowledgeable knack for what you lack

You don't want to be packed with pride

it smacks your senses

to make sure you're on track

it attacks your abilities

So you can bounce back

        The comeback is always better

because you cut back what you don't need

You get yourself back

        Setbacks helps you stand back

        so you can see the bigger picture

        You'll see the impact

TEST

We all complete tests where there are no grades

No one tells you if you've passed

but you'll know if you failed

ZIG ZAG

Progress doesn't move in straight lines

                    it zigzags

But we're all expecting an ascending

                    straight line on a graph

WIN WITHOUT BRAGGING

You can stop battling yourself

Win without clapping

Win without slacking

Get cracking

Or lose

                    without crying

COMPLIMENTS

Wear compliments like a vest

Separate from the body

but close to your chest

BE LOVE

Life is not about finding love
it's about being love

Being alone is a gift
being present with yourself
going back to your roots
grounding yourself
It's a dedication to yourself
a commitment to your heart and its contents
It's anchoring yourself

Being challenged
become who you want to be
show up for yourself
Be confident
feel free

To learn how to take care of yourself

Protect your heart
stand up for yourself

Being vulnerable

to be tender
to understand your soul
to reclaim hope and joy
Be your own saviour

Rebuild
Adapt
Mend
Walk away

Be kind to yourself
to heal

UNDERSTATED

Beautiful things don't ask for attention

They just get it

because it's special

It leaves a

          lasting impression

on you

PURPOSE

Fall in love with your purpose

it's earnest

It can make you nervous

because it goes

        beyond the surface

to develop

        you as a person

CLIFF

When your mouth

                is a cliff

Words

        jump

from your

                lips

HEALER

maybe the reason you keep attracting broken people is because you're a healer

maybe you keep attracting people who are living their nightmares because you're a dreamer

maybe the reason you keep attracting followers is because you're a leader

maybe the reason you keep attracting listeners is because you're a speaker

maybe the reason you keep attracting doubters is because you're a believer

maybe people keep finding you because you're a keeper

HEARTLESS

I am not   heartless

I just learned how to use my heart less

I realised it was

                                            priceless

AWAY

Grief

      hugged me and

            I cried

                 until

                     the loss

                               went

                         away

FALL ASLEEP

Sometimes all you can do is lie in bed
and hope to fall asleep before you fall apart

That's when you wake up, consider it a fresh start
Sometimes life gives you a jumpstart

which means it time to restart

This time you're going to take part

not be a spare part

                              Either way, you're still a work of art

TAKE YOUR LIFE BACK

We are more than the mistakes we make

Believe in yourself

Empower your confidence

There are things that break you

the past doesn't set the pace

Familiarity keeps you warm

     Grow

     Plant yourself

Sometimes your heart pounding

              in your chest

                 can be a nice reminder

             that you are alive

be curious about your compass

you owe it to your potential

take life back a little bit every day

Life should you grow
Life should move you

Rise with conviction and passion
Be proud of yourself

MUSEUM

A poet is a museum

    You put everything on display

      People walk through

        Moved by what they see

          the bravery

            the rawness

              It makes people think

ABOUT ATMOSPHERE PRESS

Atmosphere Press is an independent, full-service publisher for excellent books in all genres and for all audiences. Learn more about what we do at atmospherepress.com.

We encourage you to check out some of Atmosphere's latest releases, which are available at Amazon.com and via order from your local bookstore:

In the Cloakroom of Proper Musings, a lyric narrative by Kristina Moriconi

Lucid_Malware.zip, poetry by Dylan Sonderman

The Unordering of Days, poetry by Jessica Palmer

It's Not About You, poetry by Daniel Casey

A Dream of Wide Water, poetry by Sharon Whitehill

Radical Dances of the Ferocious Kind, poetry by Tina Tru

The Woods Hold Us, poetry by Makani Speier-Brito

My Cemetery Friends: A Garden of Encounters at Mount Saint Mary in Queens, New York, nonfiction and poetry by Vincent J. Tomeo

Report from the Sea of Moisture, poetry by Stuart Jay Silverman

The Enemy of Everything, poetry by Michael Jones

The Stargazers, poetry by James McKee

The Pretend Life, poetry by Michelle Brooks

Minnesota and Other Poems, poetry by Daniel N. Nelson

Interviews from the Last Days, sci-fi poetry by Christina Loraine

ABOUT THE AUTHOR

Charnjit Gill has an MA in Creative Writing and a BA in English Literature & Creative Writing. She is also a private tutor and is a spoken word artist. Her work has been published in the London Spoken Word Anthology 2015-2016 by Gug Press, Typishly, Minerva Rising Press, From Whispers to Roars, KYSO Flash, Ghost City Press and San Fedele Press. You  can follow her on Twitter @CharnjitGill1 and on Instagram @cgillpoetry to see more of her work.

Lightning Source UK Ltd.
Milton Keynes UK
UKHW010028190820
368421UK00001B/62